Y9/5

C000257171

POEMS BY JOAN INGILBY

Joan Ingilby in 1962. *(Photograph by Mark Gerson.)*

POEMS

STRANGE PLACES

RHYMES FOR CHILDREN AND OTHERS

BY

JOAN INGILBY

WITH DECORATIONS BY MARIE HARTLEY

First published in 1994 by
Smith Settle Ltd
Ilkley Road
Otley
West Yorkshire
LS21 3JP

© Joan Ingilby 1994
© Illustrations Marie Hartley 1994

All rights reserved. No part of this book may be reproduced, stored or introduced into a retrieval system, or transmitted in any form or by any means (electronic, mechanical, photocopying, recording or otherwise) without the permission of Smith Settle Ltd.

The right of Joan Ingilby to be identified as the author of this work has been asserted by her in accordance with the Copyright, Designs and Patents Act 1988.

ISBN 1 85825 037 4

British Library Cataloguing-in-Publication Data:
A catalogue record is available for this book from the British Library.

Designed, printed and bound by
SMITH SETTLE
Ilkley Road, Otley, West Yorkshire LS21 3JP

Contents

STRANGE PLACES

RHYMES FOR CHILDREN AND OTHERS

Preface

As a child Joan Ingilby wrote poems, but probably did not write them down, so that none has survived. The ones in this collection date from 1933, when in that decade and the following three she composed many poems preserved in thick exercise books. Joan was then living in the family home, North Deighton Manor near Wetherby. The house, its large garden and the surrounding rural countryside on the edge of the vale of York are the background for much of this early work.

In those days she bought anthologies, many published in the 1920s and 1930s, at second-hand bookshops, and in time amassed a large collection of these and the works of many poets. She felt drawn to John Clare, Emily Brontë, Wordsworth and Walter de la Mare. D H Lawrence influenced her choice of subject such as flowers, the rhythms of Edith Sitwell's poetry entranced her, and the poems of W H Auden, Robert Frost, and Wilfred Owen's war poems were favourites. For a few years she was a member of the Poetry Society.

She has in her possession, passed down in her family, what is known as the Shelley brooch, not a valuable piece, but it was given by Shelley to his cousin, Harriet Grove, and was inherited by Joan's mother whose grandmother was a Grove. Even so she prefers Keats to Shelley.

This collection falls into three parts. The first and much the longest consists of nature poems, others influenced by the times, and many expressing thoughts about them. The second short section contains poems on foreign places, whilst the third which is for children and others offers light-hearted glimpses often in the realms of fantasy.

Although she never sought much publicity, some poems were printed in *Country Life*, *John O'London's Weekly*, the *Yorkshire Post* and the *Dalesman*. But when Joan moved to the Dales to collaborate in writing books on Yorkshire there was little time left over for poetry, and the bright flow ceased.

Sea Dreams

All in the house sleep peacefully, but I
At this cold hour of the grey dawn
Can hear the seagulls' cry,
Piercingly forlorn
As inland from the sea they fly.

The rustling of their swift on-rushing flight
On wings like wind-swept sails
I greet with glad delight,
It never fails
To spurn the terrors of the night.

Their calls bring echoes of a sun-clad rock
Washed by an ever changing sea.
Their sad shrill whispers mock
Enticing me
With tales of a mermaid's silken lock.

An ocean tang is left upon my lips.
Long after they have flown away
I dream of mighty ships
Of silver spray
And sunny isles where night is day.

1933

The Wind Song

The wind cries
The trees wail
Black branches sway
In the rising gale.
Clouds scud by in a grey-green sky
The old gate creaks and the hedges sigh
The wood moans
The twigs crack
White puddles shine
In the muddy track
Dead leaves fall on the crumbling wall
The horses stamp and the sea gulls call,
The fence shakes
The wires swing,
Toadstools grow
In the emerald ring
Autumn colours cover the land
Caught in the wild winds pulsing hand.

1933

1934

You bring grim greetings Nineteen Thirty Four
Distrust, uncertainty, fear,
Unrest and hopeless talk of war
Poor innocent New Year.

When will the angry frightened nations cease
To hate, quarrel and strive?
Will blind humanity find peace
In Nineteen Thirty Five.

1934

Llewellyn Powys

The spirits of the downlands are his guides
Wandering through the ages
Ghosts of unbridled storms, encroaching tides,
Animals' and birds' cries,
Forgotten sentences and sighs
They also lived in pain and through his eyes
Reflect upon these pages.

1934

The Gardener

He loves the trees,
The frogs, the birds and humble bumble-bees.
He understands
The winds that blow
His dainty, fragile lilies to and fro.
His gentle hands
Tend well the seeds
Protecting them from choking weeds.
For he is wise; like the butterflies
He spends the hours
Between the dawn and sunset with his flowers.

1934

The Silver Birch

The prettiest tree I ever did see
Spread her leaves like a canopy,
Shielding a little lonely lane
From the cold wild wind and the cutting rain.

Her comeliness and natural grace
Expressed her love from stem to base,
Love of the earth and love of the sky,
Love of the stranger passing by.

To find her again I have often tried
Roaming over the countryside
But not one sign in all my search
Have I seen of that dainty silver birch.

1934

Michaelmas Eve

This cool September evening, distant hills show
blue and grey.
The clouds are slashed with orange where the
sun pursues his way.
A pheasant calls from covert
And rooks caw from the trees.
The harsh refrain of a passing train
Is brought by the gentle breeze.
Rabbits chase each other
And beneath the grasses lie
Mushrooms curled like silver pearls
Under a gossamer sky.
To-morrow frosted cobwebs will be outlined on
the yews
And autumn will be stepping into summer's
vacant shoes.

1934

Winter

I am filled with odd delights in winter:
Starry nights and the splinter
Of ice on the roof and the glitter
Of water in a mud hoof mark,
The twitter of sparrows,
A rook's slow 'Kark'
As he flies above mist wet meadows.
The warm glow after climbing a hill,
Firelight, and tea.
By my love for these I know
That winter will
Be filled with odd delights for me.

1935

Escape

Out of my strength shall come forth words
Out of my strength shall come not failure
Failure and weakness withdrawn
I shall publish my strength
And be contemptuous.

I shall be quiet listening
I shall think deeply of goodness
Say nothing, ignore time,
Live not dependent on the passing chaos,
I shall be free to linger.

But I shall miss the summit
I shall fall short
And slip back baffled
Even as others of more perceiving nature
Have lost their balance in Eternity.

1936

Strange People

They speak of things that I have never known
Experiences that never have been mine —
Meaningless to me
Their words are blown
Through their lungs,
Intoxicating their tongues
Like wine.
Are they free
Has each a separate soul?
Or having fought
Life's battle, after the rout
Have they merged whole
With but a single thought;
What about me
Why — Why am I left out?

1937

Gossip

Has each pavement an eye,
Like a fog light
Directed low
To catch unwary feet
Of passers-by?
Shall we suddenly know
That an invisible ray
Is watching as we go
Across the street?
If this is so
And they can talk
What shall we do?
I shan't walk
In the town. Will you?

1937

Cadogan

See how Cadogan broods
In egg-like corpulence.
Yet with what elegance
Her spout protrudes
How noble her stance
Pink cherry-eyed
Despite her laughter,
She's not too dignified
To hold hot water.

1937

Dreams

In waves of sleep
Like a sea full of fishes
Glimmer and leap
Old thoughts and new wishes.
Lightly they glide
Through the ocean of brain,
Float up with the tide
But sink back again.
Often they splash,
Incongruous streams
In a blinding flash
Of coloured dreams.
Some reach land,
But carelessly break
On the dreamless sand
Of the shores of wake.

1937

Clocks

We are bound by clocks,
Surrounded by constant ticking.
Seconds and minutes
Checking our actions.
No hoarding of hours in a box,
No distractions
Will stop their recording.
Yet if all clocks were broken —
Works and glasses —
We shouldn't hold time
For time passes.
Clocks are only a token
Bought and sold.
Clocks stop, but we still grow old.

1937

Insomnia After Driving

I cannot sleep
For if I close my eyes
A ribbon of white
Road runs into the distance.
If I open them
I see a vast expanse
Of blackness splashed with light
From a chink in the curtain
And hear the sharp cries
Of a bat out in the night
Pierce the stillness.
There is no chance
Of sleep until my eyes and last
Remnant of tired brain
Have ceased to see the glare of the past ten
  hours
And finished living them over again.

1937

I Love The Quiet Lands

I love the quiet lands
That speak no words,
The earth which understands
The songs of birds,
Where forest trees and flowers
And grasses grow,
Where coloured showers
In streams and rivers flow,
Where downland hills
Bend long, strong arms
And windmills turn by flat-land farms,
And deep red beech rides
In October,
And ploughland and plover.
All these I love,
The brown moorside,
The blossom grove
And muddy Norfolk tide,
Sweet water meadows
Glossy green,
The filtering shadows
In between
Bee covered limes,
Tracks in the mist
Which climb and twist
By cold round mountain tarns.

And I love stubble,
Thatched barns
And the bubble in the middle of a spring,
And the aching calls
Of a curlew on the wing
And grey stone walls.

1937

Showers Over Moors in June

When yesterday we walked together
Along that track across the heather
Do you remember how we heard
A melancholy crying bird
Brown of feather?

And how like other storms that pass
The rain left drops upon the grass
And the grey moors looked grimly through
The mist, then turned a starry blue
With patches of bracken freshly green
Shimmering, I have never seen
Such a bright mass.

1937

The Dales

He who would know the Dales
Should go there in winter
To see the plum-coloured bracken
And feel the sting of the wind on his cheeks.
He should walk by a cold tarn
With snow about him,
And watch buzzards
Circling the hills
Beyond the valleys.
He should go there of course in summer
Too, and sit by a clear stream
Where a dipper pokes and pries
Into the gurgling water,
And dances from stone to stone.
He should learn to train his eyes
To look to far horizons
And pick out on the skyline
A flock of sheep, a dog, and a man.
Above all he must love silence;
For he who would know the Dales
Must often walk alone.

1937

Watendlath

Whenever there is a misty day
In September
I shall remember
Watendlath as it lay
Silent and grey
The yellow reeds in the tarn
And a bracken stack
Near the barn.
The track up a ridge
On the fells,
A flock of sheep
Pushing through a gate
Over a stone bridge
White Aylesbury ducks
Huddled in a strutting bunch
And how you sat
Silently
Gazing over the water at
Nothing as we ate
Our lunch.

1937

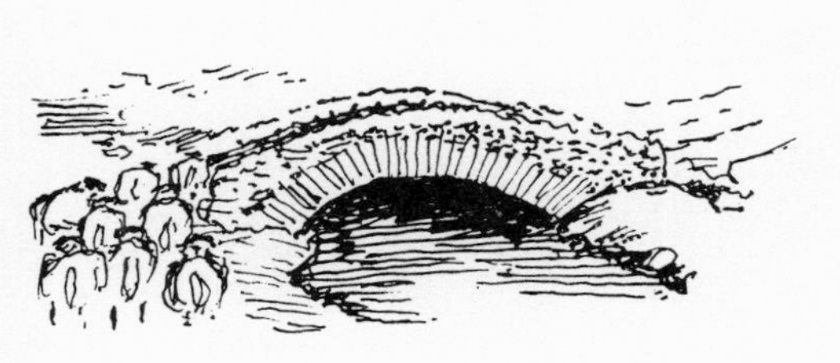

When We Break Free

We shall go singing
Down the ages
Out where the great winds blow.
We shall laugh and dance
And when a storm rages
Ride on the lightning bringing
Comfort to those below —
Those we have left below.

We shall never come back
For our spirits
Shall cleave to endless light.
Only when the leaves fall
Shall we think and smile
And call, call, call
All night
To those that we used to know —
Those that we used to know.

1937

Wagtail

Hop, look, run-run-run
Black and white
Wagtail in the sun
Up! down, turn, fly
Flickering kite
On a string in the sky
Jerk! slip!
Flap of the tail,
Lashing whip
And flying sail.

1937

Dandelion

Round each throat
A petticoat
Frilled and neat,
A golden gay
Reflecting ray
From the sun's heat,
That folds up
Like a cup
All the dark night.
But lies a flat yellow mat
In the daylight.
Thus a dandelion passes
All its life amongst green grasses,
In dusty lane and dirty town
Looking up and pointing down.

1937

Cranesbill

Brown bees caress
Your soft blue satin dress,
In sympathetic love
They lightly rest,
Tenderly pressed
Against your smooth
Fine veins of mauve,
From so honeyed a breath
Loath to move!

1937

Bedstraw

Fluffy, winged Bedstraw
All clustered spangles
Covers the floor
In flustered tangles,
Only a seeded, golden mass
Like coins from a purse
All spilt on the grass

1937

Poppies

The scarlet-headed poppies go
Nodding their heads — they know, they know
To and fro
They sway and blow.
Other flowers may also grow,
But none of them will ever show
High or low
So bright a glow.
As the corn lands
Firebrands

1937

Meadow Sweet

Feathered down of foaming cream,
Fragrant
As summer's first day,
Rippling, vagrant
As a stream
In latticed lace array
Meadow Sweet
Is frothing at my feet
Like scented spray.

1937

Tormentil

Tormentil — Tormentil
Straggle and creep
Out in the grass,
Where the grazing sheep
Trample and bleat until
They sleep.

Shining eyes
Glide over banks,
Who can despise,
Or fail to give thanks
When they pass
By meadow and hill
Where brightly lies
Yellow tormentil?

1937

A Lament For The Passing of Winter

There are no
More footprints in the snow
Now winter's gone
No blue-black trees
Against an opal sky
No flooded lands to freeze
And skate upon
And geese no longer cry
'Honk!' in the night,
We have gained the hum of bees
But lost firelight.

1938

The Lower Reaches of the Wharfe

Clear stream of infinite romance
Buried in fire at sunset,
By what unlucky chance did you get
So sullied, what dire accident
Has turned your radiance
Into a mud churned channel?
You were bred in the hills
To sparkle with purity.
On what sullen offal have you fed
For such a gross maturity?

1938

Dipper

He curtseys good day
For he's very polite
He's dapper and gay
And his waistcoat is white
You can see him alone
On his stretch of the beck
Firmly perched on a stone
With submerged head and neck.
As he looks for a worm
You may creep very near,
For his greatest charm
Is the absence of fear.

1938

I Know a Place

I know a place where hunted things may go,
Where animals creep silently and breathe,
Where fishes swim for ever in the flow
Of deep waters.
And birds frightened of noise
May stay in quietness.
Where tired men and women
Are not driven,
But rest at ease
And the sun shines on them.
If you have also found it
Tell not of it
In case others seek it not for solace
But for gain.
For then it would vanish.

1938

Leaves Have Infinite Leisure

Leaves have infinite leisure
To lie and think in the dust.
They whirl in a dance for pleasure
Yet do it because they must.
For the wind is stronger than they are
And sweeps them off the ground
Into the wavering air
With a scrunching paper sound.
Wet leaves caught in a drain pipe
Sigh for their youthful spring,
But next year when the time is ripe
They won't hear the thrushes sing,
Nor envy their new green brothers
The feel of a bird's light tread,
For they like so many others
Will be dead.

1938

Primroses

Last night wrapped in taffeta hoods
Primroses sprinkled the banks and woods,
Cut and designed from that yellow sheet
Where green from the sunset and blue sky
meet.

As dew on grass their scent is sprayed
On earth, in air, over stream and glade.
Even as blackbirds were born to sing
So primroses herald the birth of spring.

1938

Days

There are days
For walking
Up track,
Over boulder and grey stone,
And for watching the sheep graze
Quietly, and days
For talking
When the haversack seems light.
There are days
To be alone
Crusted, wind black,
Like unknown
Chasms
There are wide days for elaborate plans
And for encounters,
Or slim days
Leading to dates
Grim and crackling
But they pass
Like grain through sacking
And the haze
Of distance from a mountain.

1939

Rainbow Weather

A fine fresh feather
A-flash across the skies
And there's rainbow weather
In my eyes.
Stiff white seas roar
And gulls on curved wings soar
With wild pale cries.
There's a squeak of wet leather
And a smell of blue smoke
And long potato pies,
The shadow in a puddle
Of a solitary rook
And there's rainbow weather
In my eyes.

1939

Villanelle

Before you down your tools and die
You never are too old and frail
To set your standard in the sky

These days it's hard, but why not try
To pin it up upon a nail
Before you down your tools and die.

Much easier to listless lie
Than all alone to breast the gale
To set your standard in the sky.

Once gone you'd not regret and I
Should watch you proudly cleave the trail
Before you down your tools and die.

And like an eagle upward fly
With freedom from this earthly goal
To set your standard in the sky.

Life is a fight you must not cry
That 'All is lost' or you will fail
Before you down your tools and die
To set your standards in the sky.

1939

Alone at Night

Alone at night
I have felt the security of a car.
In the searing wind — whistle of tyres upon
  tyres
And the rhythmic throb of a well-conditioned
  engine
Steady headlight lamps
And serenity, comfort and peaceful response
To touch.
Does seductive clicking mechanism
Fold itself into a pad-like narcotic?
Black trees hold no horror
And the eyes of a deformed beggar
Pass unnoticed.
But at the slightest check,
The slowing up for corner or steep hill
The outer world becomes real again.
Turning wheels soothe frayed nerves
But if stilled suddenly
They become a menace
And thoughts race round in their place
Until the calm voice of a friendly greeting
Softens the jingle of silence.

1939

Sparks From My Fire

Have you no inner spirit,
No fire behind your eyes?
Have you no thoughts that glitter
Like stars in frosty skies?
I have a beam of colour,
A flight of shining birds,
A memory of hillsides
And a stream of intangible words.
I have heard the dawn chorus,
Seen cobwebs in the dew.
Take these from my store, I have others,
And may they comfort you.

1939

Where My Love Lives

Steep high as the wind let us go up there
Where my love lives

No slanting path leads down to damp despair
Where my love lives

The people are good and true and rare
Where my love lives

The false ones cannot breathe the air
Where my love lives

Come for there is happiness to spare
Where my love lives.

1939

We Didn't Understand

Yes — we looked at the view
The glory of Devonshire
Touched the bracken and saw the redstart.
But we knew
Something hung there in the silence
For our spirits were invisibly burdened
By the ominous prelude of the days to come,
For the ghost of war was crossing the heavens:
But we didn't understand.
For all we saw
Was a lovely June morning
And a grand
Panorama of a view
We didn't understand the warning
But our hearts and our souls, they knew.

1939

Enemies

1st Voice Courage is never lost
For the wind of life is there
2nd Voice Yet that wind can blow
Heart blinding snow
That drugs the inner ear
1st Voice But go — now — go
Stay not to count the cost
For you must mind
That shrivelled core
Of courage that is not lost
Go — now — go
Before you are totally blind
Think of great things in front.
2nd Voice No
For what is behind
I can forget
It is what may never be
And why I am
And what may upset
My little soul
That troubles me
1st Voice You have denounced yourself,
Up with that soul on high,
Be not put down
By a rotten world
That is afraid to die

Next time
You see a sneering face
Think if it as dust
Smile and ignore it, let your heart
Harbour no rust

2nd Voice What if I'm lonely
Ill, poor
And old?
I am afraid — afraid — afraid.

1st Voice Then do something — gold
Is not a necessary store.
Drag up your spirit
From the shade
Your courage is not lost
But smothered in day ghosts of
the night

2nd Voice My Dreams?

1st Voice Yes, you made them your enemies
Now you go and fight!

2nd Voice Fight them — ?
They are my life.

1939

Curious Things

I crave for curious things:
Come bring me filigree wings,
A five-sided tower,
A flower from Fingal's Cave
And seven strings,
Sweet singing clocks
With white fur doors,
The core of Vesuvius
Bejewelled kings
And strange, far stranger things
Balanced on rocks.

1939

Summer is Over

Apple tree, apple tree, sing me a song
For summer is over and winter is long,
Your arms hang heavy with fruit, your leaves
Are touching the ground like green lace sleeves.
At noon from your branches a robin sings
Has he not told you secret things?
That the swallows for the last time play
This even, tomorrow they'll be away.
Of his nest in the stone of the broken wall.
That starlings chatter of nothing at all
Of the break in the sky where the golden sun
Pours on the earth her benison.

Or are you with fruitfulness replete
And marked you not the garnered wheat?
Nor noticed when the warblers went?
Nor heard the rooks in parliament?
And heeded not the wasps that clung
Your rosy, ripening store among?
Heard not each dull, soft, thudding sound
Of 'dimicks' dropping to the ground?
Tomorrow a basket I must bear
And rob you of all you prize most fair,
But 'neath the harvest moon tonight
Bedappled in its mellow light
Apple tree, apple tree sing me a song
For summer is over and winter is long.

1939

The Mist-Swept Soft Horizons Know

The mist-swept soft horizons know
The coming of the sun, the snow,
The sleet, the hail,
The shredding rain
And the long smoke trail
Of a slow goods train.
The water tower, the single pine,
The stunted shrub, the sharp incline,
The ring of trees and white-washed home
Round funnels above rough sea foam.
The aeroplane, the swaying hawk
And shivering stars in the dark.

The mist-swept soft horizons know
The spirit of all winds that blow,
Their depth and force, their scent and sound
The different textures of the ground.
The storm clouds in the sunset light
The shadow of a winter's night
The avenue, the long straight street
The laden cart of golden wheat,
The old grey horse, the man, the plough
The mist-swept soft horizons know.

The tall church spire, the chimneyed mill,
Each dear, peculiar-shaped hill.
A glinting river, a shine of glass
From a window and every ride of grass.
The pylon line across the downs;
The hazy smoke above dark towns.
Where night furnaces angry glow
And the long indescribable flow
Of men and women in despair
Whose spirits flutter in the air,
Clutch to tumble or spring to rise
They see it written in their eyes
Which soul must stay and which may go
Those mist-swept soft horizons know.

1939

Summer Time Ends

The jasmine hand across my window
Stretches downwards straight and still
Held by a myriad tiny threads
As though against its will,
And away below
In the garden the dahlias hanging heads
Are roped together with tiny strands
Traced in the night, by dew dropped hands
Tied into their beds.
I cannot see the trees at all
An invisible cloak is theirs.
Over the fields the pewits call
Like ghosts of transient cares
But against their weird weeping springs
A robin's jaunty pipe
He does not cry on sweeping wings
For the wheat is stacked and the fruit is ripe
Despair his voice transcends
Surely no bird but a spirit sings
Such a vision of shimmering joy it brings
Though today Summer-time ends.

1939

The Wind

Who's before the wind? — leaves a' bluster
What's before the wind? — creaking mill
All before the wind? — full sails straining
Braced before the wind 'till the wind falls still

Who's in the wind? tearing voices
What's in the wind? cockle shell seas
All in the wind? rain lines glistening
Tight in the wind and the shrieking trees

Who's against the wind? — tumbling seagulls
What's against the wind? — back blown spray
All against the wind? crumbling windows
Each against the wind in a different way.

1939

Sea Song

Sad, sad sea —
Gulls swinging overhead,
Yellow-backed waves on aquamarine,
The sand and me and the bread
I am throwing the gulls, their keen,
Pale eyes of no emotion
Fixed on my hand. Their ocean
Cries of cold delight
Hang heavily pierced with lead.
Though I be free as their wings, tonight
My heart lies dead.

1939

Colour Will Flourish

Out of the density colour will clamber
Flowers but sleep in the earth,
Under the snow pale blue and amber
Crocuses struggle for birth.
Under the snow aconites garlanded
Frilled as the fringe of a palm,
Push their cold noses metalled and branded
Seeking the sun, and the calm.
Blackbirds courting above them
But never a blackbird sings
For the touch of the wind that loves them
Has frozen their ruffled wings.

Yet out of this density colour will riot
Green will inherit the ground.
All that was blank, opaque and quiet
Flourish with colour and sound.
Trembling lambs bewildered bleatings
Sweet pink blossoms hang gay,
Larches and wrens inspired greetings
Will shower the land on the first of May.

1940

The Butterfly Raid

Gaily they floated over the barley,
Backwards, forwards
Hedge top and field.
'Plague of white butterflies'
Murmured the poppies,
Forming together a banner as shield.
Whispering like women's
Long fluttering garments
In some hot country
The bent barley swayed
Crowded and hot 'neath
The cloudless horizon,
Simply ignoring the butterfly raid.

1940

Memory

I always forget from one year to another
Red berries and buttercups,
The scent of roses,
The first pale beech leaf
And torrid stripes on tulips.
I forget laced branches 'gainst a winter's sunset,
The sweet warmth of hay
And long shadows.
I forget frosted cobwebs
And bees humming in lime trees,
The steel cold bluebells
And poppies in hot corn fields.
I forget fog filming across roads,
Snowdrifts up walls
And breathless quiet before thunder.

But I remember
The sadness of lapwings in the meadows
And a wren on the pergola
Pouring his heart out into our garden.
I remember too corncrakes jarring amongst the
 wheat.
I remember digging snow in my shirt sleeves
And picking wild daffodils
That slid like a gold ladder
To the stream,

And I remember
Snatching at red leaves,
Brown leaves and yellow leaves
As hurled by a high wind
They surged out of reach.

1940

Think Not With Longing

Think not with longing of the past
Nor yet the future.
Seek not a beginning nor an end.
Trust not the present as an outcast
But gather it to you as you would a friend
That you had lost
And found again at last.

1940

Choice

Follow customs and live in confident repose.
Flaunt originality
And lose society's hospitality.
Choose either,
But do not dither and do neither
Unless you would be
A valueless nonentity.

1940

The Sea

I have not forgotten the sweep
Of the sea
Nor the swoop of the wing
Of a gull,
The sigh of the wind and
The white spray keep
Company in my heart and lull
Me to sleep and sing
Of beautiful stones ashine
At night,
Of moon pathways of
Leaping light.
And across the sand
Weed red as wine
With purple and black shells intertwine
All glistening, wet and cold,
But always my over greedy hand
Outstretched to take
But clasps a fold
Of blanket and as I spring awake
I travel sixty miles inland.

1941

Lilies of the Valley

It is an old custom in France to send a bunch of lilies of the valley to the one you love on May 1st. If you no longer send them you are said to have ceased to love that person.

You have always given me lilies
Since we were young and gay.
Will you still bring me lilies
Next year on the first of May?
Though our spring time passion is ended
And our blood runs thin and cold,
Yet you and I are blended
In love though we be old.
Should lilies fill the markets
I could not bear to see
Those bunches for the picking
And not a one for me.

1941

Sight

Stretch forth your eye to distance,
For colour muzz them slow,
Pierce them with steel by rivers
Where the bright waters flow;
Shade them against the light of the sun
And glistening frosted snow.
On misty days spread wide your eyes,
Lay them against height,
Let them breathe great depth deeply,
But rest them through the night
That you may gain a fresh surprise
At the miracle of sight.

1941

The Road to Marsett

Beside the road to Marsett
That lies in Wensleydale
The round bedappled water blobs
Their pools of yellow trail.
By the beck that runs through Marsett
I've seen a dipper's nest
And on flat stones
By the twisted bridge
Two sandpipers at rest,
And curlews, curlews calling
Their soft enquiring cry
And martins wheeling, skimming
In the misted evening sky.
And then by Semerwater
I've stood until the dusk
Has blotted from the hillside
The farms of Stalling Busk.
Straight from the chill of midnight
The birds and land and lake
I've gone to bed half dreaming
Yet wide-eyed lain awake.

1941

Rhyme For A Windy Day

When the smoke goes up the dale,
Then the cold is going to be cruel.
The east wind waves a lashing tail
Throw peat on the fire for fuel.

When the smoke goes down the dale
And softly the warm sun smiles,
Hang your coat on the back door nail
And walk the moors for miles.

When the wind from the north bears down,
Shut all your windows tight
And watch the stars spread their sequin gown
About the sky at night.

If south winds in winter blow
Clouds up like a goose's feather,
Then watch for a heavy fall of snow
And gather your sheep together.

1941

Harvest

There's a swing through the field like a stiff silk
dress
(Rustles the barley at wind's caress),
Whilst proud-eared wheat in high disdain
Withstands all winds (yet bows to rain).
And the dancing oats of the afternoon
Scarce breathe by night 'neath the harvest
moon;
Yet before another blackberry sky
In flickering flames give place to dusk
Light hearts within dark barns shall lie
And yards be strewn with vacant husks.

1941

Epitaph

Here lie a singing bell,
A flaming candle,
A heather tuft,
A vision and a cry;
A sail, a standard
And a tear for parting
A wish, a will, a messenger, But I
Left them there
And gradually they rusted
The web of life they wove withered and died,
Buried my heart beneath the cold confusion
Like wreckage flicked and tortured by the tide.
One day someone may
Pick about the pieces
Find skeletons of beauty
And exclaim —
'Here was a hope
Why was it left to moulder
Given no soul, no freedom and no name.'

1941

Rowans

Wild rowans of the Border
Ledge perched
Above Hell Gill,
In swinging pools of colour
Their clustered bubbles spill,
Where free from the clear wind
That tears up the dale
Past High Hall,
Past High Way,
Curlews call
In the day
And at night sheep
From the pastures baa!
Till a Shaw Paddock cock shrills
As dawn flushes the grey lands
Flecking the walls and hills
With pink and streaking the dim sky,
And billowing clouds
Take flight
Above where valleys darkly lie
Beneath their flock of white,

And clinging drops
In a shroud
Of mist glide
Down them from the tops,
Till the sun lighting the fellside
Spans river, field and copse.

1941

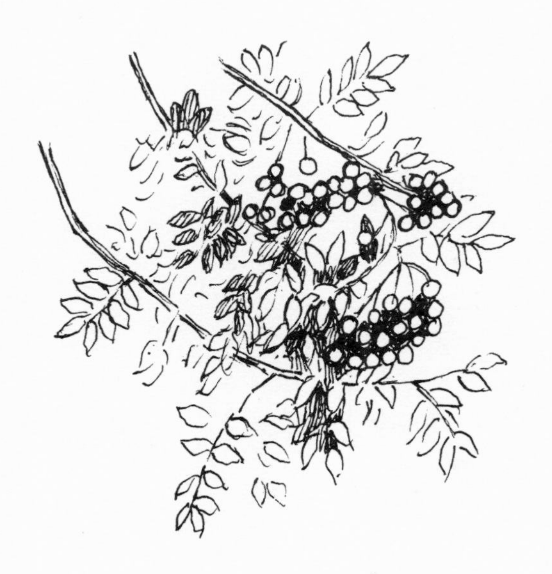

Faith To Sing

A bird in a cage,
I saw him as I walked in.
I looked again,
A thrush in a cage.
Then he began singing,
Singing!
Did he know how they sing in the woods
In the gardens?
He thought he did it so well,
He preened his feathers
Head on one side.
What a travesty of a thrush
This thing in a cage!
And yet, he wasn't miserable.
How can I explain?
He was proud
Of his piping.
His pathetic half-open beak
Whispering forth
What should have been
A clangour of sound
His poor budgerigar chirrups
Filling my soul with pity,
Pity but admiration too
For this rare indomitable spirit
Singing from the heart,

This prisoner with the faith to sing,
Who had no prospect of a mate.
He had had none for years.
He only knew
That song rose in this throat
And that he must fling it up
Into that dark shop;
And as I opened the door
He hopped from his highest perch
To tell me
(What I, free as I was,
Had failed to notice)
'Spring, Spring, Spring — is in the air!'
Thus was I shamed
By a thrush in a cage!

1942

Fishing

There are many ways of fishing,
But when you're old and wise
Tis then that you'll be wishing
You'd always fished with flies.
There's nothing like the perfect cast,
There's nothing like the play
Of a fighting fish and you've got him fast —
It's the evening rise and it's May.
The swifts chase up the river,
It's warm and the sun quite gone.
Only the reeds shiver
And the moths have come
Out in the brown twilight
To flutter about your head,
And you stare out into the night,
'till the spell is suddenly dead,
And you put up your rod, fold your net
And know that your feet are wet.

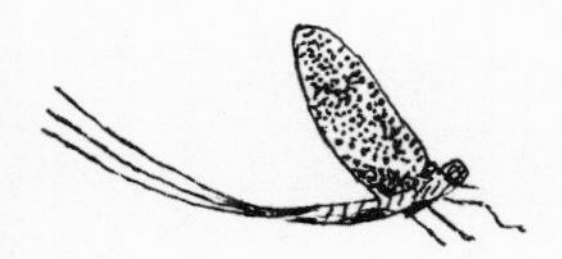

1942

Eyes Of My Heart

I can see the steel of Semerwater,
Steel shot through with purple light,
Yellow reeds with stranded shadows
Curlew calling and duck in flight.
I can see a floating diver,
Hear an owl in the distant trees,
Watch a wriggling narrow river
Ruffle in the slightest breeze.
I see marigolds at Marsett
Honey-like cover the shingly sand,
Hear in the dusk a redshank crying.
I've lost my heart to a piece of land.

I can sit on stones like sphinxes
Watching the night creep round the lake.
Fish all day in its icy waters
Offering flies no fish will take.
'neath Addlebrough's windswept shoulders
Cows file for a mid-day drink —
I've drowned my eyes in a splash of colour
Piercing the heart of a bowl of ink.

Grey stone walls the only shelter,
Fine the hay and lush the grass,
White the crested waves at evening,
Pink the sun on the climbing pass.

Snow lies long in the highest hollows,
Heather's black as the winter's late
Postman misses, milk's undelivered,
Sheep to be rescued, but few to skate.

I can hear the white duck quacking,
Feel the feather mattress bed,
Taste the fat of home-cured bacon,
Wensleydale cheese and new baked bread.
Deep within the kennel barrel
Old Floss pricks her silky ears,
While the room grows hot and dusky
(Sickly hot when the lamp appears).
At Low Blean 'neath sloping meadows
By Semerwater I went to stay
And I left part of my heart for ever
Over the hills up Raydale way.

1942

Edinburgh Castle

Edinburgh Castle was written for my father for Christmas 1942. He had told us that as a young man in the Gordon Highlanders he had sometimes been stationed at the castle and what fun it had been.

Do you often remember champagne and light
  laughter
Gay colourful waltzing, polka and reel,
The swing of the kilt, the squeak and the
  clatter
Of harness and leather and shine of bright steel?

Does blue smoke at evening or wail from sad
  pipes
Entrap your heart in a deep splitting crack?
Does a certain scent or taste twixt your two lips
Carry you forward or waft you back?

Does a smile or gesture or odd name recall
To your mind, long forgotten, a memory lost?
At the back of your eyes, does a uniformed tall
Figure take shape and then fade to a ghost?

Do you often remember champagne and light
  laughter,
Gay colourful waltzing, polka and reel,
The swing of the kilt, the squeak and the clatter
Of harness and leather and shine of bright steel?

1942

Scarborough in November

The roofs were old harbour red
And the haze chimney-pot blue
The sand mellow as harvest.
Tide-flattened stretched anew.

Gay pebbles and clinging shells
On smooth bronzed marbled rocks,
Imprisoned emerald bracelets
Of tangle weed locks

Gulls swooped like swift flung living
Steel daggers in the light
Swung up from the waves and over
Spring balanced into flight.

Above the bubbling spray
That skipped and cried aloud
A fisherman stood watching
The billowing snow flood.

And vagrant battered trawlers
Quietly passed by
To out where (like shawls of the Shetlands)
Mist wrapped the sea and the sky.

1942

Travel Bureau

There are lots of ways to travel
And this is how it's done —
You may catch the Moon Express by night
Then change to the Morning Sun.

You may leap on the North Wind Special
If your destination is far
There are lots of brilliant
Stations
And every one a star.
There's the Comet Line for a crisis
And the birds run a company too.
The silver spray of the Wavelet Way
Is a lovely tour to do.

There's a local called the Leaf Glide
That runs at the end of the year.
At Christmas the popular Royal Slide
Goes straight to the stratosphere.

In spring there's a Primrose Pleasure
Boat and later over the sea
Flies the Through Migration Airway
With season tickets free.

I can tell you how to travel —
Don't pack or move or pay.
Just shut your eyes for a moment
And let yourself drift away.

1942

Christmas Day 1942

Shall all the tea time hours
Pass on before you
Like cast-off friends you long ago forgot,
Or all the posies of sweet scented flowers
Gathered together in a single plot?

Shall only the perfect minutes, you remember
As being something precious
Small and quiet, flicker in the ray
Of the firelight of December
The twenty-fifth — Christmas Day.

The tall grandfather clock
Now crowned with holly
Knows secrets, but tells nothing but the time,
If it could speak what brittle words could flock
From that melodious chime?

Now we are gathered round
About the fire,
No lights, but the red apple wood flame,
No-one says anything aloud,
But the air is full of meaning just the same.

Future and past are always blent
With the present,
This year their smouldering embers fitfully
  burn,
For some from the past are absent
And in future may never return.

1942

On reading an account of 'The Old Oak at Cowthorpe' written by Thomas Maude, 1774 or 'The Oldest Vegetable in the world'.

But 'Children of the forest' seem other oaks to me,
Of storms of weather and wars of man,
What have you seen since you began
To grow into a tree?

One thousand years ago, did a little acorn sprout?
Who saw your first proud foliage break,
Who watched that none should touch or take
The little seedling out?

I only know your guardians of very much later date.
Snowsdales, Hammertons, Stourtons have been
Your landlords, but they have only seen
You in a declining state.

If only I could have known you in your
  upstanding prime,
    As though in some bewitched glade
Stand under your half acre shade
    Thrown over space and time.

Full twenty-seven yards measured your trunk
  around.
    Only an eighteenth-century storm
Did you any permanent harm
    Man dealt you not a wound.

But now of your ancient body, spread-eagled,
  shrunk and curled
    In the field, these words are the poor best
I can say 'There lies the oldest
    Vegetable in the world'.

1943

Northerner

I belong to the lands of the North,
To the wind, the snow, and the gales.
I'm at one with winter's wrath,
With the stones and soil of the dales.
Whose long broad-shouldered hills
Bring tears of love to my eyes,
Like a roaring spate down the gills
Or a rainbow lighting the skies.
To float on the waves of content
I shall not need a blue patterned sea —
A moorland flecked with cotton grass sails
Is freedom enough for me.

I shall travel abroad to the South,
Enjoying the soft café days.
I shall taste strange food in my mouth,
And watch foreign people and ways.
I shall thrill at each sound and sight
I shall reach for the sun though it burn;
Until, in the cool of one night
I shall know it is time to return.

1943

Butterfly

How you have wasted
This short spring day —
Thrown it away —
Like blossom-fed wind
Slinging petals and all
Of the foaming cherry
Over the wall.
While bees, sweet-laden
With stolen honey,
Creep from the coffers
Of golden money.
Take wing! Take wing!
For life like the spring
Is gossamer quickly shed,
And a shadow falls so easily
On a butterfly that's dead.

1944

Easter 1944

There are lots of things to remember
About words and feelings and sights,
And time is a sea of the future
With islands of hidden delights.

There'll be a new September
For me, and a Spring for you
Lots of things to remember
And hundreds of things to do.

1944

'Snowflake'
(Snow Bunting)

You have come to us,
To us in this little village
You who have travelled beyond the perpetual
snows.
(According to Linnaeus)
The only living bird that knows
The frozen North. Fed upon saxifrage.
Bred in a rocky crevice,
Your nest lined with the hair of a reindeer.
You have traversed
The ocean to visit us here
You stayed not on our Eastern seaboard
As your wont:
But pushed on inland
Born on the wings of a storm.
You strayed from the band
As they fled before the wind.
Their white tails flapping
It was kind
Of you, but you shouldn't have left the lapping
Sea, the luscious weed,.
Here you will find
Only a little grass seed.
I heard your mellow notes
As I walked in white fields

And felt the gate, crisp
Beneath my fingers
Little wanderer — the place yields
Poor living
There is only a wisp
Of straw for your comfort, do not linger
Go — This place is not for you, fly away.
Away to the sea
Your friends will be giving
You up — Yet if you leave me
Now, my heart will go with you —
To Lapland or Hudson's Bay.

1945

English Earth

A wild duck scutters to the shore
And rooks fly over by the score.
The grass is covered by beads of dew,
The sun is faintly breaking through
Like an apricot veiled in filmy lace
The water mirrored in its face
A swan, like royalty, sails away
Across the farthest reeded bay.
Now Highland cattle graze the scene
Where usually only deer have been,
And ancient oaks placed here and there
Give to the park a solid air
Of having always been the same —
From forest land with royal game
To grass and then to earth that now
Bows to the tractor-driven plough

The lord of the manor free to roam
Across the land that bounds his home,
May be a symbol of the past
And of his kind perhaps the last.
It does not worry him as he
Walks homeward round the lake for tea
Though all the parks in England may
Be turned to public profit they
Will never lose their ancient charm

While bordered by manor house or farm
Or proudly terraced castle wall
Or moated grange or haunted hall,
Old families have had their hour
Soon other hands may seize their power
But whatever be their breed or birth
They'll be English men tilling English earth.

1945

Celandines

These little yellow flowers of spring
Can teach our generation much.
They do not fear the atom bomb,
They only hear the mistle thrush.
They turn their golden cups to catch
The early dew and face the day
With glistening petals like eyes that snatch
Their liquid from the blackbird's song,
Their colour from a rainbow's ray
And life from a martin's wing.

1946

Faces Unaware

Out in the street
The people go
With dragging feet
Or sprightly toe.
Here is sorrow
And seldom joy
Save in some little girl or boy.
This bag is heavy,
This woman ill,
That man's worried
About the mill.
A laughing party
Of chattering girls,
A rich old woman buying pearls.
A pensive youth
In his uniform
Dreaming poetic
Thoughts — still born.
A heavy mother
With aching corn
A slatternly drudge
Her buttons torn.
A clerk, hair oiled
Pin stripe — tight waist
A blonde, hard boiled,
Red-lipped to taste

A cleric passes
With thin, drawn friend,
To take some classes
Or attend
A dreary meeting
Where words drone flat
Each a pale face 'neath a black hat.
There are hungry eyes
And bored good looks.
A hundred mysteries —
Lords and cooks
Heroes and heroines for a novel,
From castle, flat and rural hovel
Up the street
The people go,
With dragging feet
Or sprightly toe.

1946

Sympathy

A tender smile, a turn of the head,
Not the words, but the way they're said,
The lowered lash over softened eye
Swift as a shadow the wind blows by —
Thus have I known sympathy.

The gentle touch of a passing hand,
No need for words if you understand
The spirit behind the body's wall
Where thoughts flash fleeter than kestrels fall —
Thus have I known sympathy.

1950

Haytime

I would show you them —
The hills — through my eyes today
With the folk in the meadows strewing,
Strewing the hay,
Rhythmically moving up and down.
I would send the sheer breath of the country
To you in the town.
White gulls are dipping,
Soaring out there on the breeze
Over crested grass like waves rippling
In warm summer seas.
O! I would send you these today —
The peace of the hills, and sweet on the wind
The scent of the hay.

1950

The Narrow Way

I never go blindly forward without knowing
The possibility of fear.
I touch my heart and whisper, 'You are going
To where the tempter mocks the naked ear'.
I tell my secrets in the market-place
That I may look my demon in the face.

If I can but see the evening approaching,
Gallant with armour bright I'll stay,
No indecision o'er my course encroaching,
But like a sunshaft pierce the narrow way.
I'll turn the mirror to my faltering eyes
That I may penetrate my own disguise.

Self-knowledge gleams like a sword to guard
the wearer,
Lose it and you lose the road as well,
Struggle in life's darkness lonely wayfarer,
And fall where other blinded travellers fell.
I try to grasp the hilt with my whole will
And hope some day to breast the summit's hill.

1950

Awareness

May I always take my part.
Let no cloud unwrap my soul, smother my heart
Lest ideals that once seemed clear should fade;
And jettisoned, leave my life a masquerade.
The chorus of fear and pain —
That rhythm which haunts me again and again
Like the lilt in joy, we should all hear;
Guilt lies on those who close one eye, block one
ear.

1950

In My Garden

I know it's not the thing
To confide,
But really in spring
I did have some pride
In my garden.

By summer, well I own
That the weeds
Had certainly grown
Better than the seeds
In my garden.

And wasps and birds enjoyed
All the best
Apples, then destroyed
Plums with equal zest
In my garden.

At Christmas came the snow,
I thought that
It would never go;
Everything laid flat
In my garden.

Yes, this year, I confess
I do feel
Just a little less
Glamour and appeal
In my garden.

1950

Train, Train In The Valley

Train, train in the valley.
Your song, your shuffling shafting song —
'I'm hurrying up, I have to go on,
I'm hurrying up, I have to go on' —
As if you were quite near,
As if before long
You might appear beside me.
Then that choked breathing of yours
Seems suddenly to fail,
Get faster, then fainter,
Get faster, then fainter,
And you're off up the dale
Just a puff of smoke in the valley.

1950

A Tender Thing

Easy it is to hurt a tender thing —
Insect with gossamer wing —
See, the first buds of spring
Bruise in the wind.
Each human heart is laid
Open to be betrayed.
We must be kind
As the sun is warm.
How gently our hands should move
Towards the ones we love,
To do no harm.

1950

The Unconquered

Free as the clouds above me
That feather the spacious sky
I'll lift my thoughts from blunt despair
And curve them up to the buoyant air
Where swifts in ecstasy fly.
Steadfast, I'll spend my fancy
On nothing that's mean or base.
I'll take my strength from the storm-lashed
  hills,
And rest on the wind whose passion fills
My heart as it strokes my face.
My limbs my servants shall be
Whilst ever my lungs draw breath,
As lightning's scimitar slits night's vein,
My spirit's tilting body's pain
Shall shiver the spear of death.

1950

Winter

Wind's thongs sting the heather now
Where streams drum in the gills.
Rain turns to sleet and storm tears flow
down the bleached hills.
Bare trees sway and chips of light
Flicker on barns and walls.
Then softly, softly through the night
The white snow falls.

1951

Devotion

My heart has never been whole
Since I first heard a nursery rhyme,
And its lilting magic stole
My love for all time.

Bright words float over my brain
Like sunlight on the blade of a knife.
Trying to catch their refrain
I blunder through life.
Yes, words are my sole desire,
But when taken to use as I would
In a sacramental fire
They burn my heart's blood.

1951

The Poet

My prisoner voice there's no locating
'Till I burst the band
That is suffocating
Words I must say.
Only a pencil turning, turning
Here in my hand
Like a cinder burning
My thoughts away.

1951

Village Before Dawn

However well you know a place
It looks different
At three o'clock in the morning,
When the houses have their eyes shut still,
And the stones are unresponsive.
No smoke plumes gather about
A single chimney,
And mists are down on tree and hills
No children shout
There's not even a window-shrouded face.

Until five,
The church clock marks the minutes
With no-one there to see;
For this is the last breath of night,
A silver cobweb-time as it were,
All silence and mystery;
Before clinking milk pail, dog's bark,
Or voice from an open doorway
Salutes the dawn and puts to flight
The fragile fingered shadows of the dark.

1951

Loneliness

They laugh and talk as usual, how can it be?
I watch them as if breathing different air,
While grief stands by me
Like an empty chair.
Even home and loved possessions tend
To mean nothing: Only
The absent friend
Is everywhere. That's what it is to be lonely.
O, how tragically easy to forget how to feel
Love, delight and sorrow!
Time, they say, can heal,
But how different to have faith in any
 tomorrow!
Yet, solace there is in unexpected places,
We're not too far apart
For kindness in strangers' faces
To penetrate the chasms of the heart.

1951

The Key To Spring

As we grow older every year
Spring music strikes more sweetly on the ear,
And as the fires of winter cease to glow
And the dread winds no longer cruelly blow,
Venturing out, we welcome with fresh surprise
Each sign of a new birth that meets our eyes.
Some, such as sticky chestnut buds
Or dog's mercury in bluebell woods,
Seem ordinary, though none the less
Part of spring's fearful joyousness.
How wonderful the growth and hue
As leaves and petals surge anew;
Yet I feel locked in winter 'till
Over pasture, moor and hill,
While sunlight stains the dry stone walls,
A solitary curlew calls.

1951

Watching

It was night, and the stars
Hung over the fells, and
My eyes burnt with watching;
'Till morning shadow,
Smoke, and another day's
Gate unlatching
Scattered the dusky hours.

1952

Happiness

Delight — a fast vanishing thing
Like a rainbow after a shower
Has a delicate transitory ring —
A quality rather than power.
Happiness lies in the heart
Its roots are set firm and deep.
I enjoy delight as an art,
But am sometimes so happy I weep.

1955

Invitation

When clouds enfold the hills
And the becks pour down the gills
Come out with me.

When rushes creak and sway,
And meadows are sweet with hay
Come out with me.

When sun dapples the leaves,
And the ripe wheat stands in sheaves
Come out with me.

When the earth wool-wrapt in snow
Acts foil to the fire's glow
Come out with me.

1952

From One Old 'Un To Another

I can remember when eggs were only the
second course at breakfast
And silver (cleaned once a week) lay on the
dumb waiter.
How can we know what is going to last
What anything may become later?

In those days exercise was necessary, so we took
a walk,
Or lazily lay in bed behind the drawn curtains.
When conversation is bottled in telephone talk
Little is permanent and nothing certain.

Red flag, red tape, youth dreams of narrowing
space.
When we were young the earth seemed vast,
and reasonably free;
But youth experiments by making its own pace.
Come! take a jog-trot with me.

1955

The Canal

Mud squelches no longer under the weight
Of heavy horses. Silence is broken
Only occasionally. Each lock gate,
Still easy, swings open
But seldom, especially in winter. Trees bleak
As their keen edged shadows
Etched black on grey water, creak
As a sharp snow-laden wind blows.

A solitary boat aims for the white
Stripe marking the channel on the stone
Bridge, where usually the bright
As a rainbow kingfisher darts alone.
Ahead, reeling in hastily, a fisherman pauses
To raise his hand as the boat passes, saluting
  canals
And perhaps all lost causes
Before mist blots him out and dusk falls.

1960

Exile

This was home: the little pond,
The stone house, the long walled
Garden, the pasture, with beyond
It, the moor where in spring the curlews called.

All the noises there rang true,
From the cock crowing at first light
To the ceaseless gale that blew
Roughly against the window panes at night.

If a leaf fell from a bush
It could be heard to caress the breeze.
On summer evenings a thrush
Or blackbird sang 'till dusk from the damson
trees.

Rain brought out the becks in spate
Whose pluming waters streaked the fells.
Wild was the roar, as desolate
To hear as echoes trapped in cold sea shells.

Silent as the driving snow
That bared the tops and filled the track.
Obliterating time I know
Sweeps forward. I will not look back.

1961

Country Childhood

Gathering fruits and flowers
We passed exquisite hours.
Daisies lay in warm wet hands
That next day reached for willow wands
But learned not to touch
The trustful robin's clutch.

First buds were enchanted,
Not that they weren't wanted,
Only hallowed. It was when
The fields were strewn with gold that then
To a lone cuckoo's calls
We wove the cowslip balls.

Every high summer
We tasted tips of clover,
Smelt the scent of new mown hay
That in the curving windrows lay
And heard above the stream
The swift's shrill scream.

We, like the greedy rooks,
Haunted the ripening stooks
Where the pimpernel shone bright.
Then, when evening turned to night,
Or after dawn had come,
We brought the mushrooms home.

1961

Look Forward

'Look forward not back' you said
Forward to what, old age,
To the Time when only food and bed
Seem important, when no rage
Rises, and hearts no longer burn
With the saving wish to learn.

1961

Truth

Truth can seldom be told
Lately we found
A neighbour so poor and cold
That we had to rush round
And get a paraffin stove alight,
Or she would have died in the night.

Truth can rarely be spoken,
James 'passed on,'
(As if he were a token).
Friends said 'He's gone
Before.' They never mentioned he died.
Yet, can it be said they lied.

Can truth be known now
Since all our senses
Have been forced to grow
To man defences?
How many people still care
Or wish to be fully aware?

1962

Inspiration

Where does inspiration hide
Who knows, who knows
As moved by a strange capricious tide
She swiftly comes and goes.
Time has no grasp on her,
Thought is her slave,
She holds reason prisoner
And gives us all we have.
To he who woes her most
Appears she last;
For he has in his ardour lost
The one he loves the most.
In case she knocks in vain
At a closed door,
Never a sudden thought disdain
Or a sound ignore.
She casts away despair,
Reproach and hate.
So buoyant be, with mind aware
And heart at ease, await
The sudden surge of wings,
The melting of the bars
Before the spirit upright springs
To mingle with the stars.

1962

Wind

Cruel the crash of wind above sea,
Slash and creak,
Wreck and shriek,
Wind above rough sea.

Fickle the voice of wind in the wood,
Crack and break,
Bend and shake,
Wind in the dark wood.

Secret the sign of wind against wall,
Whistle, frisk,
Snarl and whisk,
Wind against cold wall.

Gentle the grace of wind in the grass,
Weave, caress,
Wave and press
Wind in the soft grass.

Mighty the force of wind across plain,
Blow and sweep,
Lull and weep,
Wind across vast plain.

1962

Season's Child

O, I would climb the ladder to look
At onions lying on the loft floor,
Smell their succulent scent
And listen to their dry skins rattling
On the dusty boards.

But blossom caught me unawares
And sunlit hours slid idly by.
All I could see was blue sky and hear singing
High up there a lark.

And I would watch the weighed down branch
Of a loaded tree in a plum year,
Note how bloom on the fruit
Is worth the care and resolute picking
Of warm soft flesh.

In the golden years of well-propped sheaves,
(With scarlet pimpernels underfoot)
Clear up over the stooks
I'd fling my body, running, running, springing
As straw pricked my legs.

And in cabbage-time when fields were full
Enveloped in leaves I'd be walking,
Hear the cautioning crunch

Before the splash of the outpouring
Crystalline dew.

O, I would slice the cold blocked snow,
Azure shadowed like my blue shirt,
Sweat in the magical sun,
And finish with the first star blinking
At the lonely moon.

1964

The Star Gatherers

Sometimes I see them there,
The grave star gatherers,
Picking the Pleiades before my eyes.
What do they need them for,
To light a banquet
Due to break up before moonrise?
Sometimes they fail to come,
And stars jostle
Each other across the heavens
Spark by spark.
Sometimes they take them all
And for good measure the moon.
Primaeval fear still lingers in the dark.

1964

The Footpath

In earlier times the children
Came this way to school,
Their voices ringing through the thin
Air like ice on a lake
When the thaw begins.
They used to run down the
Meadow footpath in single
File, laughing and shouting,
Tossing their heads as they went,
Swinging satchels,
Light of footstep.
There was all the world
Still to be met head on —
So many first times still to come.
There is only one child now
In the hamlet. She leaves for school
In her father's car.

1982

A New Old Saw

A pasture with nettles is a pasture gone down;
A pasture with thistles will have to be mown.
Sweet herbs in the meadows bring good farmers
fame;
But meadows with ragwort bring bad farmers
shame.

1955

STRANGE PLACES

Ajaccio

The old face
Of a woman
Under her black wool shawl
Creases in kindly wrinkles
As she calls
In argument with another,
The streets are full
Of people crushed together
On the pavement.
Laughing, shouting, to each other
Under the palm trees
Out in the square
With the statue
(Which only visitors notice) where
The boys play football
And the water
Gushes from a spouting tap.
Everything is so bright,
Life is only possible
Where there is sun
To stroke the pastel
Houses and light
The brown eyes
Of the men.
Here mongrel dogs lie
Like round balls in the dust

Children run and when
They are tired sleep
Because they must.
By a corner the grey
Coated knife grinder
Sits under a yellow
Umbrella sharpening
His blades,
He wears a Turk's cap.
An odd fellow
With a devil-may-care
Attitude, wanting
No clients, minding his own affairs,
Plying his trade
In solitude.
Farther up the road patient ponies
Stand waiting,
They wear bells on their harness
And draw two-wheeled carts
Bright with blue,
Orange or yellow wheels
Red-headed whips
And checked rugs,
Driven by drab coated
Quiet men
In clean threadbare velvet.
Here an officer in khaki and red cords,
There a fisherman mending his net.
By the quay —

A bar tender in white apron
Carrying drinks
To brigands in red sashes —
And a gay voice sings
Full throated serenading
The day
The Mediterranean
And the women — mingles
With cries
Of the town and is drowned
By hooters and mule bells
All sweeping
Together into an ecstasy
Of white hot sound.
Plane trees cast their shadows
In cool patches on the pavement,
And a breeze laden with scent
Of orange blossom
Caresses the air.

1937

Lizard

Swift, shy lizard
Poised head erect.
Eyes rolling a-dazzle in the sun
Watching some insect.
Little green dragon run
And hide under the flecked
Shade of a shrub's shadow,
Glide that no human eye may detect
Whither you go.

1937

Night Sounds

Through the long hours
Of the Corsican nights
I hear the motor boats
Chugging out in the bay
And the lights
From the hotel drive flicker
Under my window
Cocks crow suddenly
Or a reveller sings
And nightingales with moonlight
Silvered wings
Fill the garden with melody
Here in Ajaccio
Such sounds flow restlessly
'Till at dawn they mingle
With children's screams
And the jingle
Of mule bells in jangled unity

1937

August in Ostend

Pink Children
In yellow bathing dresses,
Bright red, bright blue
And speckled bathing dresses,
Pink children
With happy faces,
And grown-ups too
Gentile and Jew
These you will find
In August at Ostend.
A jovial band
May be at the races
Or Casino
(If they've got some brass to spend)
Or sending coloured post cards
To a friend.
Out for a row
Or just
In cosy heaps upon the sand.
Where bathing huts
All painted bright
With numbers and stripes
All green and white
At crazy angles stand.
Here people bathe,
Upon their right

A long curved pier
And on the left each circling wave
Licks courteously the promenade
Whose stones rear
Arrogantly near at hand
And a guard boat stoutly manned
Stands by.
While under the clear sky
Fathers sleep and Mothers rest,
Nurses call and children fall
Retreating before the tide,
Or sit
Just thinking it grand
To be at the seaside
Getting nicely tanned.

1937

Visit To America

The rhythm of New York
Sounds like giant's footsteps,
Yet like many outsized people New Yorkers
Are light on their feet
As — WALK, DON'T WALK
(Quick — quick — slow)
They glide, wave-like
Under green and red lighting,
To peremptory sirens and
The moan of more ordinary traffic.

When we said 'Thank you'
The reply was 'You're welcome'.
This quite automatic rejoinder
Brought a flush of pleasure
To the face and we felt good.
They felt good too no doubt. If we said so
They'd only answer 'For Heaven's Sake!'
And hurry on with their questions:
Did we like the city
And what would we buy if we had the money?

This was a difficult question
To answer. They couldn't or wouldn't
Believe that in what they think of as

Poor little England sunk in poverty
Practically anything can be bought —
Except the moon — which we don't require.
We remarked that a barrel of Macintosh Reds
Pulled straight from the trees in Vermont would
  please
Us most. They laughed and said again,
'For Heaven's Sake!'

They looked at us as if we were
Beings from another planet. The English
Are rare in New York. A couple
Rushed up to us in the teaming sweaty
Port Authority Bus terminal
And cried, from their hearts,
'You're English. We come from Lancashire.
Where do you come from?'
Surely the desert and Times Square
Have something here in common.
But in New York the facts that elevators
Are natural phenomena,
That cab drivers do not know the buildings
In their own city, that doormen and
Hotel porters are not interchangeable,
That iced-water is not an affectation
But a necessity of life, that
Walking a block takes longer than
You think, and that tipping is nothing
But a reflex, and lessons soon learnt.

We told them that New York made us feel gay,
  young
And rather light-headed.
Quite seriously, they replied that
We had drunk too much coffee.
'Could be' we said, eyeing with some
Distaste the proffered half-cold so-called
Tea. How we laughed and talked
Far into the night! 'We're so happy'
We said. Uncertain suddenly lost,
They queried 'Is that right?'

It was odd to be so foreign in such congenial
  company
Nothing is more foreign that the same
Language not fully understood.
If we could meet not only
In hospitality and with searching words,
But with understanding, like meeting anyone,
However dislikeable, from our own country
When we left they said,
'Have fun'. We did. But it wasn't altogether
For fun that we went to America.

1965

RHYMES FOR CHILDREN AND OTHERS

Riding Will

Over the moors and up the dale
The wild wind whispered a stirring tale
Of Skipton Road and Trollers Gill
Of the coal black mare and 'Riding Will'.

Friend of the poor, this rider bold
Relieved the rich of their bags of gold.
Patrolling the lonely roads at night
He downed the wrong and upheld the right.

These desperate doings brought him fame.
Where did he live? And what was his name?
In York they dined and drank their fill
Toasting the highwayman 'Riding Will'.

While in the midst of everyone
Nevison who was the doctor's son,
Winked as he sat amongst them there
Drinking the health of his own black mare.

The Governor of the prison went
One moonlight night on his pleasure bent
Ready with wine and pockets well lined
When a black masked man rode up behind.

'Sure and it is the hand of fate
Meeting your honour out so late'
The governor turning in surprise
Gazed on a pistol and mocking eyes.

Loud he swore as he shook his fist
'For the evening's work your neck shall twist'.
From the ruins of the disused mill
Echoed the laughter of 'Riding Will'.

The governor got the sheriff's man
And that's how the midnight chase began.
Before they went the governor said
'Capture the fellow alive or dead'.

Clickerty, clickerty, clickerty, clack
Full twenty-five men upon his track
'Will' with his face both firm and pale
Rode for his life through the 'Striding Dale.'

Hot was the gruelling pace he set
'Come up old girl, we shall beat 'em yet'
He coaxed his mare as they topped the hill
''Tis neck or nothing' said 'Riding Will'.

They reached a gap dangerously wide,
She gallantly took it in her stride
Crossing the gorge so rocky and steep
Known to this day as 'Nevison's Leap'.

Then in the darkness loomed the wall
And friendly gates of Percival Hall
Quite safe from pursuers in their lair
Lay 'Riding Will' and his coal black mare.

1933

Ducks

Squabbling ducks,
On toad-like feet,
Ruffled feathers
And searching necks
Swaying and strutting they
Pass in a file like a crocodile
Of gossiping school girls.
Over the grass
To the narrow stretch
Of water that curls
Like a snake on the land
By the sunken hedge,
Each wobbling body
On reaching the edge
With flapping tail, sets a jaunty sail
As light as a ketch.

1937

Rabbit Flurry

Go out and watch the rabbits
For they've got enchanting habits
And I've never known this recipe be wrong.
When you're not feeling fit
Go and watch the rabbits sit
Your nerves will seem comparatively strong;
For they'll — skid across the grass,
Skip above the grass,
Leap against the grass.
Worry, hurry, scurry
It's just normal rabbit flurry
When people like you and me pass.
To the brow of the hill
They'll not come back until
Long you have lingered there silent and still.
Then up will pop an ear,
A nose will next appear
And then an eye, a body and a tail.
Forgotten all their fear
They won't notice that you're near
Quietly sitting with your back against a rail
Now this should show to you
That rabbits worry too

So like them try your troubles to forget,
Although they live to eat
They beat worries with their feet,
No one's managed to exterminate them yet!

1939

Poseur Our Cat

Upright before the branching fire sat
Poseur our own inimitable cat.
His deep eyed long mock-penetrating gaze
Sunk in the crackling fury of its blaze.

Each pale unflinching orb reflecting light
Like stars twinkling on a moonless night.
Only his tail twitched restless in a curve
Vitally expressive tight-sprung as a nerve.

How great the thought behind those solemn
eyes,
Resplendent, studious, how refined, how wise!
But on a sudden, I regret to tell
At the same moment as the dinner bell
Was rung, a black streak hurtled round the door
And Poseur posed no longer on the floor.

1939

Mate To Missus
Christmas 1942

Mr Mate ‘Let me in, let me in,
Let me in, I say,
Let me in at once as
I have much to do today’.

But the door wouldn’t open
And the window stayed shut
The fire blazed up
But Mate said ‘Zut’!

The more the fire blazed
The more his tail twirled
He laid back his ears
And mewed a naughty word!

Mr Mate ‘Let me in, Let me in,
Let me in, I say:
Now you can’t tell me Missus
You’ve forgotten Christmas Day!

I’ve got a present for you
Have you got one for me?
Is it partridge or parsnip,
Or cream for my tea?

— No? Well I never heard
Of such an awful thing,
To pay you back I'll shriek at you
The carol we cats sing!'

Miaow! Miaow! Miaow!

1942

A Doggerel Rhyme for a Wensleydale Pony

She is ours is solid Dolly
How we love her ample girth,
Strong of body, sweet of nature
Dale her breed and dale her birth.
Dappled grey that sturdy figure,
Flourishing mane and tail of white,
Pricking ears yet sweet demeanour
Pride of our hearts, she's a lovely sight!

She is ours to love and serve us,
Ours to deck with harness new,
Ours to feed and ours to care for,
Ours to brush and ours to shoe.
She has eyes as soft as honey,
Square but gentle woolly feet,
She's a willing, working pony
Queen of the dale, our Doll's a treat!

Down steep roads past tank and tractor,
(Dolly isn't one who cares)
Trotting with a heavy milk float
And four of us on wooden chairs.

Now there's a war she's on short rations,
Out to grass — no warm place to loll,
When she is old, we shall remember,
Love and cherish 'Wensleydale Doll'.

1942

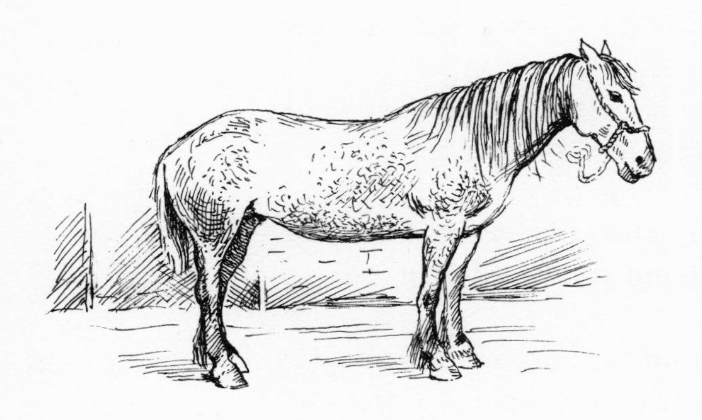

The Purple Cat

One day whilst standing in the street
A cat walked underneath my feet.

It wasn't just a common cat
I wouldn't bother you with that.

But it was purple t'was no doubt —
I shut my eyes and turned about.

But when I looked again to see —
I gazed at it, it gazed at me!

As sure as I am standing here
Its tail was purple and each ear.

And all its paws, but on its back
Were spots of blue and green and black.

Amazed — I couldn't even speak
Not so the cat for with a shriek

He said 'Come on! I want my tea'
I could do nothing but agree.

And as we went along he said
'I prefer fish and meat to bread.

I have a ration card for mice
I like my cream with nuts and spice.

Please call me as the clock strikes six
And don't forget the kindling sticks'!

I felt the hair rise on my head —
'I hope you'll like it here' I said.

My key I fitted in the door
'I know my way. I've been before.'

I went to lie down on my bed
A stone-cold towel about my head

A furtive whisper from the mat
Proclaimed to me the wretched cat

Had followed me upstairs and now
Was asking me the time and how

Would I like to be kept waiting
And didn't I deserve a rating?

I groaned and asked 'What do you need,
'A fan, a feather and some seed?'

'What for? 'I asked, in faint surprise
'To cool and then to bathe my eyes.'

Somehow under my dressing gown
I managed to get dressed, and down

The stairs I stumbled but to find
I'd left my shoes and coat behind.

But now the cat had disappeared,
And I was feeling somewhat cheered.

When with a loud and awful yowl
He entered with a frightful scowl

He said 'Why have my clothes all gone?'
I couldn't speak or move my tongue.

I'd no control of what I said —
I laughed — I cried — I ran — I hid.

I rushed outside and slammed the door
Yet still he scratched and mewed and swore.

He bit, I tugged — the door gave way —
I woke to find that it was day.

And I had fallen out of bed —
'Thank goodness it's a dream' I said.

1942

Mirabel And Mr Darcy

My name is Mirabel
Just Bella for short.
I'm a middle-aged spaniel
(They bred me for sport)
I was born (and still live)
At a large country seat.
I'd a kennel,
A keeper and plenty to eat.
Three Labrador pups
Were living next door,
We arrived the same day
And they kept us all four.

I never liked noises
I can't tell you why.
But I heard them say once
I was what's called 'Gun Shy'
So my mistress said 'Bella
Shall come out with me.
I'll speak to her gently
And then we shall see'.
She took me for walks
And she didn't mind
If I rushed off in front
Or lagged far behind.

It was one winter evening
The sky thick with snow
That she first brought me in
Whispering 'Master won't know.'
He found me next morning
And gave a loud shout.
They talked a long time
But I wasn't sent out.
And ever since then
Getting older and fatter
I've eschewed all sport
I'm not even a ratter!
I've one gentleman friend —
He's not what you'd call classy.
He's a black Persian cat
And his name's Mr Darcy.

1944

A Moral Tale In Verse For Children: Dick Duck And Frisk Fox

Dick duck was very young
When he ran from his mother
Frisk Fox smiled sweetly
And slunk up the hedge.
'Why don't we' said he
'Go off with one another' —
Enticing Dick Duck
Up to the pond's edge.

Then Dick cried 'Quack really
If you don't walk too quickly
I'd like to come with you
To see the dark wood'.
Frisk Fox gave a smirk
That to us would seem sickly,
But Dick thought him
Wonderfully clever and good.

Frisk said 'On my back
I will give you a ride Dick
Hold on to my ears
With your little blunt bill'.
And so they set off
Dick's wings like a sail spread,

The wind well behind
As they raced up the hill.

By the hedge at the edge
Of the wood, Dick dismounted
They slipped through a gap
In the broken-down gate.
But o! it was dark
And the trees closed all round them.
Dick whispered 'I think I'll
Go back now, it's late'.

But Frisk whisked his tail
Said 'You haven't seen half yet
My house is up this way'.
And branched to the right.
Dick found his small feet
Entangled in bracken —
He hurried and tumbled
And quacked with fright.

A jay roared with laughter,
A pheasant whirred skywards,
A little Jack rabbit
Bolted and squealed.
Frisk said 'Get up can't you'
And ruffled Dick roughly.
Dick wanted his mother
His pond and his field.

Then came a great silence,
Most dark and most fearful.
Not a twig cracked
And not one bird sang.
Poor Dick, out of breath,
Heard his little heart beating.
Then suddenly came
A great shout and a bang!

Frisk lay at his feet
His tongue lolling sideways,
His legs still twitching,
His eyes gleaming red.
Dick didn't know
What it was that had done it —
He only knew
That Frisk Fox was dead.

'Get into that bush'
A little voice whispered
And there beside him
A small robin perched.
'Get into that bush
You silly young duckling,
I'll take you back home
When the keeper has searched.'

Poor Dick huddled down
In the thorn and blackberries.

A big burly man
Strode up with a gun
And picking up Frisk
Said 'Got you, you rascal
Tis what you deserve
For all you have done'.

He stooped for a minute,
To look at some feathers
Poor Dick had let drop
In his struggle with Frisk
'A duck I'll be bound
You clever old devil
To get a fine dinner
You'd take any risk.'

Then straightening himself
The keeper departed,
And nothing was left
But a spent cartridge case,
Some feathers, some blood
And a wiser Dick Duckling,
A thorn in his foot
And a scratch down his face.

The robin was good as his word
And flew chirping
Before Dick and shewed him
The shortest way home.

And when Dick saw the pond,
His mother and brothers
He vowed that never no more would he roam.

1945

For Marie from Chris and Rockie

O today we feel so cocky, so cocky, so cocky
(Our names are Chris and Rockie)
We're waiting to be fed.
We'd bring you bones and rabbits, and rabbits,
  and rabbits,
But you don't like our habits
So here are licks instead!

We haven't got a present, a present, a present,
We nearly caught a pheasant
And brought it home for you,
But Rockie went and ate it, and ate it, and ate
  it,
And Chris he said 'You bet it
Would never never do!'

Joan said this card was funny, so funny, so funny,
That bone and bird and bunny
Were a thing she called 'Taboo'.
But to us it seems so rotten, so rotten, so rotten,
Looks as if we had forgotten
But you know we never do!

So paws in the air — Hens to spare
And forty-two winks for Chris.
We love you 'Hark' — you can hear us bark
Bringing our Birthday wish-!
O' today we feel so cocky, so cocky, so cocky
(Our names are Chris and Rockie)
And we're waiting to be FED!

1945

The Christmas Market

I went to the Christmas market
To see what I could buy
I wanted a stick of chewing gum
And a kite to sail on high.

I went to the Christmas market
Lit up with streaming light.
There were aisles of stalls and crackers
Chocolate and Turkish Delight.

I went to the Christmas market
The hall was frosty cold
There were tricycles and dogs on wheels,
Popcorn and chains of gold.

There were flapjacks in silver paper,
And a crown for a fairy prince.
There was pork and ham and apple jam
And cheese and cake and mince.

There were brilliant Indian carpets,
And fine soft eastern rugs:
There were pewter plates and ringing glass,
Beer mugs and Toby jugs

I went to the Christmas market
By moonlight through the snow —
I stood at the doorway watching
The people come and go.

'Twas a lovely Christmas market —
But yet I could not buy
A single stick of chewing gum
Nor a kite to sail on high.

1945

TO
THEDAIRY
SHOW
DAISY

Daisy And The Dairy Show

'I want to go
To the Dairy Show'
Tossing her head
Our Daisy said:
'I'm going to London'.
With four loud moos
She bought four shoes
From the blacksmith down the lane.
Said she 'With these
I can walk there with ease
To London and back again'.
She's determined to go
So we shan't say 'No'.
She's off today for London
Asked 'What will you do?'
Daisy answered 'Pooh,
I know my way about London.'

1955

The Larapy

I know a browsing larapy that lingers in the
 shade;
Down an ancient lane in a holly bush is the
 lovely lair he's made.
He feeds on mushrooms only,
He seeks them through the night:
To watch a larapy browsing is a rare entrancing
 sight.
Once a hundred thousand of them paced
 moonlit fields in flocks,
Their hooves all fringed with silver, and black
 their curling locks.
Tonight if you meet a larapy with his down-
 curved luminous face
Just bend one knee and bow your head
To the last of a fabulous race.

1955

Roundabout

'Old Geordie's Giddy Gadabout'
Is what I call my show.
It's the finest roundabout you've ever seen.
Won't the kiddies all come running when the
  village gets to know
As Geordie's setting up upon the green!
You see I've an eye for colour
An' ah knows what children like.
I've 'ad to modernise miself o' course.
Boys will mostly pick a motycar, a airy plane, or
  bike —
But I loves mi gold cock an' trotting horse.
I've gone around the fair grounds
Since I were six year old,
'An' now as seventy year has rolled away;
I know I much prefer the cloppin' ponies an'
  the bold
Gipsy lads to the 'Spivs' i' cars today!
But that now ain't my business,
An' the world goes round and round,
No matter what I thinks, nor if I care;
So I'm off tomorrow morning to another patch
  o' ground,
An' we'll meet again at next October Fair.

1951

LITY
JOYFUL
GADABOUT
CHIL